MW01593056

Summary of

Robert Kolker's

Hidden Valley
Road

Inside the Mind of an American Family

Intensive Life Publishing

Summary & Analysis

By

Eline Stone

Table of Contents

Note to Readers

This is an unofficial summary & analysis of Robert Kolker's *Hidden Valley Road: Inside the Mind of an American Family* designed to enrich your reading experience. Buy the original book by visiting the link or by scanning the QR code below.

https://link.intensivelife.com/HVR

As a way of saying **THANK YOU**,

we are offering a **FREE** copy of *Summary of Untamed*.

You will also be part of our **mailing list**!

Just visit the link or scan the QR code below:

https://link.intensivelife.com/free

Hidden Valley Road Summary Overview

Hidden Valley Road shares the extraordinary true story of the Galvin family, a midcentury all-American family with twelve children, of which six are diagnosed with schizophrenia. The Galvins became science's greatest hope in the quest to understand, and potentially eliminate, the disease; they were one of the first families to be studied by the National Institute of Mental Health.

The book is a captivating blend of a scientific detective story, an exciting medical mystery, a tragic family saga, and a heart-rending drama, all rolled into one.

Thanks to Kolker's incredibly intimate storytelling and character development, *Hidden Valley Road* is one of those non-fiction books that often reads a bit like fiction.

Tag along on science's quest to uncover the true nature of this puzzling disease and learn more about the somewhat dark history of schizophrenia and psychiatry. Be brought into the world of the Galvin family in a very intimate way and see the many devastating consequences that dysfunction, and secrecy, can lead to.

Hidden Valley Road was an instant #1 New York Times best-seller, and it was chosen by Oprah Winfrey as her latest Book Club Pick. She described the book as, "a riveting true story of an American family that reads like a medical detective journey and that reveals the shame, denial, shock, confusion, and misunderstanding of mental illness at a time when no one was certain what schizophrenia was or how to treat it."

Chapter by Chapter Analysis

The book is divided into three parts, and each part is made up of several chapters. Each chapter either tells the story of a specific family member, gives an overview of how schizophrenia is understood at the time, or discusses the advances in schizophrenia research.

Part 1

Chapter 1

The first chapter is set in 1951 in Colorado Springs, Colorado; it gives us an idea of what Mimi and Don are all about, namely tradition, culture, sophistication, and keeping up appearances. It also paints a picture of Mimi's childhood, which, in turn, explains why Mimi desires and values the things that she does.

Kolker starts by explaining how Mimi and Don got into falconry. A friend of theirs made it sound like an archaic and exclusive pastime practiced only by a secretive few, and as they learned about the history behind it, they found themselves fascinated. Such a tradition, especially one considered to be the mark of nobility and royalty, fed into their shared love of culture, history, and sophistication. They were hooked.

Falconry gave them a sense of accomplishment; this was in part because they found that parenting a child did not offer that. After all, taming wild birds could be brutal and punishing, but with consistency, devotion, and discipline, it was unbelievably rewarding. For Mimi and Don, the same could not be said about raising children.

Then Kolker paints a picture of Mimi's childhood. The experiences she had as a child created a desire inside of Mimi for a life that would not just be extraordinary, but also safe and secure. In 1937, she met the man who could offer her that: Don Galvin.

Chapter 2

The second chapter is set in 1903 in Dresden, Germany. It discusses the history of schizophrenia—originally called dementia praecox—and tries to explain exactly what this mental illness is.

In 1990, Daniel Paul Schreber began writing *Memoirs of My Nervous Illness* while being confined in an asylum. Up to this day, it remains the most analyzed personal account of being psychotically paranoid and wildly delusional. At the time, Schreber wrote the book as a plea for his release, but it did not turn out that way; instead, the book contributed greatly to the then-emerging and increasingly contentious discipline of psychiatry.

When Sigmund Freud finally read Schreber's memoir in 1911, eight years after it was published, he became convinced that psychotic delusions were mere waking dreams brought on by the same causes as everyday neuroses, and therefore interpretable in the same way.

Carl Jung, however, disagreed with him. At the heart of Jung's objection was the question of the nature of mental illness. Is schizophrenia something you're born with? Is it something you acquire later in life after you've been scarred by the world? Is it a mere physical affliction of the brain? Most importantly, is it nature or nurture?

By the time the Galvin boys came of age, the field of psychiatry and its view on schizophrenia was divided; some said the problem was biochemical, others neurological, genetic, environmental, viral, or even bacterial. Researchers seeking a biological key to schizophrenia were on the lookout for an experiment that might settle the nature versus nurture question once and for all. To them, a whole family of Schrebers would be the ideal sample set as it would be clear that something specific and identifiable must be happening inside some, or even all, of them.

Chapter 3

The third chapter brings our focus back to the Galvins; it is set at the end of World War II and discusses their first decade as a married couple. It tells the story from Mimi's point of view and explains the reason behind her desire for a large family, namely the feelings of accomplishment, as well as the chance to fill an emotional void to distract from her sorrows.

Over the course of several years, Don served in the Navy and the Air Force and furthered his career while Mimi gave birth to their first eight boys: Donald (1945), Jim (1947), John (1949), Brian (1951), Michael (1953), Richard (1954), Joe (1956), and Mark (1957).

The couple, however, kept growing further and further apart; even falconry, their shared passion, became something that Don did on his own.

Don was a devout Catholic, and in an attempt to bring him closer to her, Mimi converted to Catholicism. During her formation, she became friends with her tutor, Father Robert Freudenstein, a local priest. Mimi's mother questioned the propriety of this friendship, but for Mimi, Freudenstein's visits were seemingly the best part of her conversion to Catholicism.

The author also briefly discusses Mimi's parenting style, and notes that by the 1950s, the psychiatric profession had set its sights on mothers like her, calling them "schizophrenogenic".

Chapter 4

The fourth chapter is set in 1948, Rockville, Maryland; it tells the story of Frieda Fromm-Reichmann, a German-American psychoanalyst and pioneer in the psychotherapeutic treatment of psychosis who greatly changed the way schizophrenia and all mental illness was perceived in America—both for better and for worse. She was part of a new wave of analysts who were inspired by Freud and willing to gamble with their patients.

At a time when mainstream psychiatry's approach to schizophrenia was both ineffective and inhumane, Fromm-Reichmann stated that schizophrenia was curable, and those who disagreed simply did not care enough about their patients.

According to Fromm-Reichmann, people are not born with schizophrenia, but it is their mothers and fathers that are to blame.

Fromm-Reichmann had sounded the alarm over "the dangerous influence of the undesirable domineering mother on the development of her children" for years. She called mothers like Mimi Galvin the "main family problem" and came up with a term that would stick for decades: the schizophrenic mother. This term, as well as many others, helped to turn mother-blaming into the industry standard for psychiatry.

Chapter 5

The fifth chapter begins in Colorado Springs in 1958 and focuses on Don and Donald. The United States Air Force Academy had opened in their town, and Don was about to start the academic life he had longed for by joining the Academy's faculty as an instructor. Mimi, on the other hand, gave birth to four more children: Matthew (1958), Peter (1960), Margaret (1961), and Mary (1965).

When Don became part of the Academy, he took over the falconry program and completely threw himself into the job. The gap between Mimi and Don grew ever wider, and Don only saw the children when they were helping out with the falcons.

The Galvin's oldest son, Donald, was a teenager by now, and although he resembled his father in many ways, there seemed to be something that kept him from connecting with the world in a conventional way. He became moodier and more troubled as the years went by and exercised supreme authority over his younger brothers. Jim, the second oldest and less successful son, felt like he was in constant competition with Donald.

By now, the Galvin home had become a place where two different realities existed at the same time: the reality of the boys' wildness and the model family Mimi and Don believed they had.

Chapter 6

The sixth chapter begins in 1963. The family had just moved to Hidden Valley Road, a few miles out from the center of Colorado Springs; for the first time, they felt at home.

Donald managed to keep all of his inner turbulence a secret and was starting his freshman year. For Mimi, coming to Hidden Valley Road meant the beginning of her family's long-awaited von Trapp family-style idyll, but with Donald gone, the power vacuum among the brothers was seized by Jim, who was becoming increasingly wilder. All the children recognized that there was something wrong with him, but Mimi and Don were not the least bit worried.

As the 1960s progressed, the habits and motivations of the Galvin children became more mysterious and frightening to the other parents in town, but for Mimi and Don, all was as it should be as long as the children came to mass on Sundays, dressed appropriately. Coddling is something that they did not want to do as they believed that the children should be allowed to make their own mistakes and learn from them. How else were they supposed to grow up?

Chapter 7

The seventh chapter begins in 1964 and focuses on Donald's first year at Colorado State.

Here, Donald was subjected to his first psychiatric evaluation, forcing Mimi and Don to face the possibility that maybe all was not right with their son. While the first mental health professional who examined Donald found no evidence of a serious disorder, the extent of his troubles later became blatantly clear.

Donald confessed the bizarre things he had done, and it was obvious that the disconnection he had always felt was not going away at college; in fact, it was only getting worse, manifesting itself in new and frightening ways.

Unfortunately, schizophrenia was still very misunderstood and there was little discussion of a cure. Mimi and Don believed that if they admitted Donald to a mental hospital, the only certainties were shame and disgrace, and instead, they hoped that things would improve.

They managed to get Donald back into college where he kept seeing therapists. Outwardly, he seemed to be doing alright and he even met a girl, Jean, whom he married soon after.

Chapter 8

The eighth chapter focuses on Jim and details how he was starting to exhibit the same strange behavior as Donald.

Determined to beat his older brother, Jim had been building his academic record and did well enough to transfer to the University of Colorado at Boulder. There, he met Kathy, and the couple quickly got married after she became pregnant with Jim's son, Jimmy. However, the couple started fighting more and more, and Jim became increasingly more violent.

Kathy was frightened for herself and her son, but she was also terrified for Jim, who seemed tormented by something. During this time, Jim experienced his first hospital stay for a psychotic episode; although Kathy never liked Mimi and Don, she decided to tell them what had been happening.

Sadly, they did not take Kathy's concerns seriously and instead framed what was happening as a marital problem between the younger couple.

Chapter 9

The ninth chapter is set in 1964 at the National Institute of Mental Health (NIMH) in Washington, D.C. It tells the story of the Genian quadruplets and discusses the nature versus nurture argument surrounding schizophrenia and other mental illnesses.

By the time they were twenty-three, all four Genian sisters were diagnosed with schizophrenia, and in 1955, they were referred to the NIMH where they entered the care of David Rosenthal.

At the time, the search for a physical or genetic marker for schizophrenia had become outdated in psychoanalytic circles; out-argued, it seemed, by a new generation of therapists—Frieda Fromm Reichmann among them. However, many neurologists and geneticists continued the search for a biological marker for schizophrenia.

The Genian quadruplets seemed to offer the opportunity to settle the nature-nurture argument once and for all, but as the girls suffered a lot of abuse, there was no way to tell if their schizophrenia was caused by their genes or their family environment.

Even so, Rosenthal felt comfortable crediting a mixture of genetics and environmental factors for what had happened to the Genians. He rejected the argument that one single gene must have caused the illness, but he also rejected the belief that only the environment was to blame. Rosenthal became one of the first researchers to suggest that genetics and the environment might interact with each other to produce the symptoms of schizophrenia.

Rosenthal stated that future research is needed to build a bridge between the two ideas, and he was determined to prove that the wellspring of madness might not be nature or nurture, but a fateful combination of the two.

Chapter 10

The tenth chapter focuses on Donald, his visits to the psychiatrist, and his involuntary commitment to Colorado State Hospital in Pueblo.

After his wife Jean decided to get a divorce, Donald attempted to take both of their lives, but Jean managed to escape and Donald is put in jail.

Kolker then discusses the horrifying history of the Colorado State Hospital in Pueblo as well as the then-upcoming drug, Thorazine. Thorazine was seen as a sort of miracle drug that was able to calm patients out of psychosis when nothing else but shock therapy or surgery would have done the trick.

Kolker notes that drugs became the common treatment of schizophrenia but reminds us that even today, no one knows why Thorazine and other neuroleptic drugs do what they do. If we still do not have a clear understanding of the biology of the illness, is it then not strange that doctors have been treating schizophrenia pharmacologically for decades?

After cooperating with his treatment, Donald was released from the psychiatric hospital a few weeks later. Mimi and Don continued to do their best to keep up appearances, and they helped Donald find a job, but this was to no avail. His mental state was only further deteriorating.

Chapter 11

The eleventh chapter begins in 1971 and gives us a better idea of what Margaret's childhood was like and talks about how Donald terrorized the family home after his release from Pueblo.

Margaret hated living at home. The constant conflict between the boys and her mother's constant criticism disturbed her immensely, but what bothered her the most was Donald. He was now living at home more often, and Margaret lived in constant fear, never knowing what was coming next.

Jim, on the other hand, took pleasure in the whole situation. He came up with a nickname for Donald: Gookoid. The name stuck, and most of the younger siblings copied it. Teasing Donald felt better than avoiding him, which drained them of all agency, but making fun of him gave them a sense of power over a situation they had no explanation for.

Chapter 12

The twelfth chapter focuses on Margaret and Mary and talks about the sexual abuse they suffered at the hands of two of their brothers, Jim and Brian.

Jim often had all the younger boys and girls over to his house for sleepovers. And when things were too strained at home, the girls sometimes spent entire weekends at Jim and Kathy's house. Kathy was like a mother to them, but the girls were among the first to see that Jim was just as unstable as Donald.

Around the time when Margaret was five, Jim started sexually abusing her, but he was so kind to her that it seemed normal and even a little like love. Around the time when she turned twelve, she started to realize how wrong it all was and began fending him off.

Unfortunately, she did not tell anybody about what he had been doing, and as soon as Margaret refused him, Jim started abusing her younger sister Mary.

Furthermore, the girls dreaded their home situation and Donald so much that in the contest between Donald and Jim, Jim won; and they kept coming back for more sleepovers.

Kolker then explains that one of the reasons why Jim's abuse might have seemed normal to the young girls is because they had also been molested by their other brother, Brian.

Chapter 13

The thirteenth chapter explains how all of the boys are negatively affected by both of their parents. Mimi was overly controlling, and the ever-unimpressed Don was such an accomplished figure that all the boys grew up believing they could never reach his level. It gives us an idea of who the third, fourth, and fifth oldest children are: John, Brian, and Michael.

John was a devoted classical musician and did his best to stay far away from the family.

Brian, the best-looking Galvin boy, was extremely talented, but very quiet. Mimi and Don, however, were so in thrall to him that it never even crossed their minds that he might have been suffering unnoticed, just like Donald.

Michael, on the other hand, was a rebellious boy who ended up getting thrown in jail several times. He was also admitted to psychiatric wards, but Michael never thought of himself as crazy. To help him make that argument, he had the entire 1960s ethos on his side as the anti-psychiatry movement was gaining momentum. People were claiming that insane people were not insane at all and that schizophrenia was nothing but a coping mechanism to deal with the absurdity of the world.

This did not help the Galvins any further.

Chapter 14

The fourteenth chapter is set in Dorado Beach, Puerto Rico, where 'The Transmission of Schizophrenia' was being held: an academic summit about the continuing debate over nature and nurture and schizophrenia. David Rosenthal, the researcher from the NIMH who studied the Genian quadruplets, was the organizer.

Through a study that he conducted with Seymour Kety, Rosenthal discovered that schizophrenia could not be imposed or inflicted on someone who is not genetically predisposed to develop the condition, thus discrediting the idea that bad parenting created the disease.

Rosenthal thought that he had finally settled the argument and was ready to share his findings, but at the conference, his ideas were met with skepticism.

Rosenthal did, however, meet one kindred spirit at the conference: Irving Gottesman. Together with James Shields, Gottesman had just published a study in which he argued that schizophrenia could be caused not just by one gene, but a chorus of many genes, working in tandem with, or perhaps activated by, various environmental factors. Gottesman and Shields' theory became known as the "diathesis-stress hypothesis"—nature activated by nurture. Decades later, their work would be seen as phenomenally prescient, but at the time, the nature-nurture debate continued.

Because of this, families like the Galvins continued to live at the mercy of a mental health profession still caught up in a debate that came nowhere close to helping them.

Chapter 15

The fifteenth chapter is set in 1972 on Thanksgiving, a day that has extreme importance to Mimi.

The whole family was present, except for John. But before everyone was even seated, Donald and Jim ended up in a violent physical fight, ruining the entire evening. Mimi finally had no other choice than to admit that she had failed miserably, but outwardly she remained in denial.

By then, most neighbors did not visit the Galvins anymore, and children were no longer allowed to come and play. It was no longer only Donald who was troubled, but also the younger boys, like Matt, who was caught stealing, and Peter, who stuffed a girl's face in the snow and kept it there until she couldn't breathe.

However, the worst was still to come.

Chapter 16

The sixteenth chapter is about Brian's murder-suicide and the subsequent change to the family dynamic.

Here, it is revealed that Brian had been prescribed Navane, an antipsychotic that treats schizophrenia. Both Mimi and Don knew this at the time, but they would keep it a secret for many years to come. The thought of another insane son—their amazing Brian, of all people— was too devastating for them. But in 1973, after killing his girlfriend, Brian turned the gun on himself.

After this traumatic incident, the family changed for good. John moved away, believing that what was happening to his brothers was contagious, and the other sons also started to drift away.

Not counting Donald, Mimi and Don had just their four youngest children left at home: Matt, Peter, Margaret, and Mary.

Chapter 17

The seventeenth chapter is about Don's stroke, which hospitalized him for several months and led to his early retirement, as well as the effects it had on Peter, who eventually also spiraled out of control.

For Peter, witnessing his father's stroke seemed to have shaken loose whatever self-regulating mechanisms he once had, and he too eventually had to be admitted to a psychiatric ward. There, the staff soon learned about the other sick boys: Donald, Jim, Brian, and maybe also Joe, the introspective seventh son.

Several of the doctors who examined Peter seemed to blame Mimi for his state, referring her to the schizophrenogenic mother theory. After all of this, Mimi was so broken, that when she was phoned by Nancy Garen, a woman she only barely considered a friend, she broke down and told her everything. Together they arranged for Margaret to stay with Nancy during the upcoming years. This decision left her sister Mary distraught, as she was now stuck at home with only Donald and Peter for company.

Part 2

Chapter 18

The eighteenth chapter revolves around Lynn DeLisi, a female doctor and researcher who dedicated herself to the search for a verifiable neurological cause of schizophrenia.

She did her residency with Richard Wyatt, a neuropsychiatrist who explored the effects of mental illness on the brain itself. Early on in her time in Wyatt's lab, DeLisi was approached by David Rosenthal, who was still on hand as a research psychologist. He wanted to do a follow-up study of the Genian quadruplets, twenty years after the first one.

DeLisi was pleased with the chance to study the physical roots of the disease, and she decided to ask Elliot Gershon for advice. Gershon was the only schizophrenia researcher at NIMH and was looking closely at genetics.

However, Gershon told her he saw no point in studying the Genian quadruplets as they had the exact same genetic code. He wanted to study so-called "multiplex families", families with varying mixtures of the same genetic source ingredients. The more afflicted children, the better. And the key was to focus not just on the sick people in the family, but everyone—ideally more than one generation.

If DeLisi was up for tracking down families like those, Gershon would be much more interested.

Chapter 19

The nineteenth chapter tells Mary's story, specifically the time after her sister Margaret was sent off to stay with Nancy Gary.

Mary had to stay at home because she was not old enough for the private school Margaret attended, and she felt left behind.

In the meantime, Mimi had gone back to her old patterns, putting on a brave and cheerful face and demanding her children do the same. Don, who was still recovering from his stroke, was becoming restless as his falconry days were behind him and returning to work was an impossibility.

Kolker also briefly discusses Mary's relation to Jim. Kathy, Jim's wife, had become somewhat like Mary's surrogate mother, but Jim continued his sexual abuse and became increasingly more violent.

Chapter 20

The twentieth chapter revolves around Margaret's stay with the Gary family.

Like the Galvins, they were dealing with their own family illness, namely myotonic dystrophy, an incurable genetic disease. But unlike the Galvins, the Garys were extremely rich.

Initially, Margaret felt out of place, but eventually, she assimilated. However, she always kept her family life a secret to her new friends. This was possible until Matt enrolled at a private college nearby. During one of his visits to the Garys, he had a nervous breakdown, and it became clear that Matt also suffered from the same illness as several of his brothers.

To Margaret, this was her old world crashing in on her new one, a reminder that she did not belong there and that nowhere was safe.

Chapter 21

The twenty-first chapter is about Michael and his stay at 'the Farm', a famous spiritual commune founded by the counter-culture hippie icon Stephen Gaskin.

Michael arrived at the Farm in 1974, partly as a hippie in search of a new way of living, and partly because he was out of options.

While he was there, his contempt for his own family intensified. He knew he was not insane and had not gotten over how his parents once wanted to commit him to a mental asylum. When he finally returned home, things were even worse than before he left. Donald was still there, Peter was now sick too, and his father had had his stroke.

Everything seemed more out of control than he had remembered it, and he came away dejected.

Chapter 22

The twenty-second chapter gives a quick overview of all of the siblings, with Mary, Peter, and Donald being the main focus.

Mary would often visit Margaret at the Garys and wanted nothing more than to move there as well. She was now the only sane child living at home with Donald, Matt, and Peter. Matt, the brother who once was her protector, was now part of the problem.

Chapter 23

The twenty-third chapter revolves around Mary and her first year at her new school, as well as her name change.

Mary's seventh-grade application to her sister's school was denied, but she was accepted to another celebrated school far away. This was her ticket to freedom: a life without Peter, Matt, Donald, and, most importantly, Jim, the brother who had now raped her. This was something he had never accomplished with Margaret.

To make matters even worse, right before her departure, Mary was invited to a high school party where she was also raped by two boys.

Too clouded by shame, she told no one what happened, but she made herself a promise to never live in Colorado Springs again.

It is during her first day at school that Mary came up with her new name: Lindsay. A teacher told her there was already a Mary Galvin at the school and asked her for her middle name. Mary invented one that sounded nice, and from that moment on, Lindsay was her name.

Chapter 24

The twenty-fourth chapter is set in 1979 and discusses Robert Freedman's advances in his research on schizophrenia.

Robert Freedman and Lynn DeLisi had two different approaches to the same problem. While Freedman was searching for a physiological understanding of schizophrenia, DeLisi aimed to track down the genetic components of the illness. He wanted to know how it worked, and she wanted to know where it came from.

Neither of them knew that their paths would one day merge in the study of the extraordinary Galvin family and that their findings would help them unearth new knowledge about schizophrenia.

Freedman had learned that people with schizophrenia might have difficulty processing all the information sensed by the central nervous system. This "vulnerability hypothesis" was an elaboration of Irvin Gottesman's 1967 diathesis-stress hypothesis, and Freedman sought a middle ground between nature and nurture by suggesting that certain genetic traits directly compromised the brain's sensory and information-processing functions, making the brain especially vulnerable to any number of environmental triggers.

To these researchers, those triggers—anything from a heartbreaking separation, to chronic poverty, to traumatic child abuse—did not cause schizophrenia as much as providing an opportunity for vulnerability to turn into disorder. That vulnerability was an issue with "sensory gating", or the brain's ability, or inability, to correctly process incoming information.

It seemed like the problem with schizophrenia patients was not that they were unable to respond to stimuli, but rather that they lacked the ability not to. Their brains were not overloaded but lacked inhibition.

Freedman wanted to isolate the gene irregularity that caused this. If he could do that, then he would have proven the existence of a schizophrenia-related gene, and he would have opened the door to a genetic remedy. However, for this, he needed a large family with an extraordinarily large incidence of schizophrenia.

Chapter 25

The twenty-fifth chapter is about Lindsay's first year at boarding school, Margaret's first years at university, and the six sick Galvin boys.

Now that Lindsay, aka Mary, and Margaret were both away from home, they grew much closer. During Margaret's first year, she met Chris, who soon became her husband. This made her friend Wylie jealous as he was in love with her. He called her before the wedding, but Margaret rejected him; she knew that marrying Chris was the wrong thing to do, but he offered her a much-needed escape from her old life.

At this time, Joe, the introspective seventh son, had his psychotic break. This meant that six of the twelve children had fallen ill. First Donald and Jim, then Brian and Peter, now Matt and Joe.

Joe returned to Colorado Springs, joining Peter and Donald and their parents. The person who everyone was most wary of, though, was Jim. Kathy had finally left him after he also started hitting their son, and he was working less and drinking more. Nobody knew what he might have been capable of.

Chapter 26

The twenty-sixth chapter is about Lindsay opening up and beginning therapy.

During her first year at college, Lindsay started seeing Tim Howard, Sam and Nancy Gary's nephew, and started therapy with Louise Silvern. Both Mimi and Don rejected the idea of therapy, and Lindsay paid for everything herself.

After many sessions, Lindsay decided to tell her mother what Jim had done. In the past, whenever Lindsay would open up to Mimi, Mimi would urge her to move on, always reminding her that others had it worse. Therefore, it came as no surprise that when Lindsay told her about Jim, Mimi responded that she, too, had been sexually abused as a child.

After hearing her mother's story, Lindsay felt closer than ever to her, but Lindsay hoped her mother would also take her side. Unfortunately, Mimi never took the side of a healthy child against a sick one, and that was not going to change now. Instead, Mimi started talking about how Jim was mentally ill. This deeply hurt Lindsay, and she vowed to never again be in the same room as Jim.

When Jim eventually did show up at the house while Lindsay was there, Lindsay screamed at him, and Don made it very clear that Jim was no longer welcome.

Chapter 27

The twenty-seventh chapter gives us an idea of how schizophrenia is viewed at the time and revolves around Lynn DeLisi's research with the Galvins.

After three decades, the schizophrenogenic mother theory was losing its hold, and the latest DSM—the DSM-III, published in 1980—had narrowed the diagnostic criteria for schizophrenia so that it more closely resembled a specific illness, instead of a syndrome.

During this time, DeLisi had begun collecting the genetic material of families with schizophrenia, including the Galvins, who were the perfect sample. The multiplex family database greatly contributed to the body of knowledge about the disease.

In 1987, Daniel Weinberger reframed the concept of schizophrenia as a "developmental disorder". In the years to come, this developmental hypothesis caught on with other scientists. The theory suggested that to effectively fight schizophrenia, we might have to treat people before they even seem sick. To be able to do this, researchers would have to isolate the genetic makeup of the illness. More and more researchers were joining DeLisi's search for the genetic mutation.

Chapter 28

The twenty-eighth chapter gives an overview of how all of the Galvin men were doing, including Don.

Most of the sick brothers were on strong medication, and here it is revealed that Peter, who turned out to be bipolar instead of schizophrenic, was also sexually abused by one of his brothers as a child, although it is not specified which one.

The brothers who had not become sick had been doing their best to move forward with their lives, with varying degrees of success.

Don was in his sixties now, but had aged considerably more due to his stroke; he was dealing with several health concerns and had received his first cancer diagnosis. To Don, everything he had built up in his life now seemed to mean

nothing. Lindsay sometimes wondered if Don was disap-
pointed in all of them, feeling that even the six healthy children somehow had failed him.

Chapter 29

The twenty-ninth chapter talks about Margaret's life after her wedding and how she dealt with her past.

Her marriage to Chris had lasted barely a year, which greatly disturbed her, but she graduated and found an out-patient rehab to kick her weed addiction.

This was also the period when Lindsay and Margaret were closest, and they finally talked about what Jim had done to both of them.

Margaret also confronted Jim and told her mother, but Mimi reacted the same way she had with Lindsay; this left Margaret extremely angry, but Wylie was there to support her, and the two eventually got married.

Margaret tried several different non-traditional forms of therapy, and she was getting closer to healing. However, unlike Lindsay, Margaret needed to keep her distance from the family to get it done.

Chapter 30

The thirtieth chapter revolves around Lindsay's attempts to take care of her brother Peter.

Lindsay was now twenty-six. She had been seeing her therapist, Louise Silvern, for seven years, had started her own corporate event-planning business, and had a new boy-friend, Rick, who eventually became her husband. However, having such a nice life made her feel somewhat guilty, and it spurred her into helping her brothers, especially Peter, who still had many lucid moments.

She became his state-designated caretaker and did her best to help him heal. This would work for a while until Peter stopped taking his prescriptions. After some time, Lindsay had to admit that her "experiment" was starting to look like a failure.

As they were closer now, Lindsay asked Peter if he had also been sexually abused by Jim, and Peter said yes. This made Lindsay wonder why she did not become ill, as they both suffered similar traumas. Was it her brain chemistry? Her genes? Or maybe her many years of therapy?

Chapter 31

The thirty-first chapter is about Mimi and how she dealt with everything that happened.

Mimi was becoming increasingly more bitter, and when Donald confided in her that he had been sexually abused by her friend Freudy, Father Robert Freudenstein, she used the now-deceased priest as the new explanation for everything that had gone wrong with her family.

Mimi also decided to become more open about the past with her daughters. These revelations helped the girls to see their father in a different light and made them realize that they had been rather harsh on their mother. Margaret wondered if all of those traits that she had always ascribed to her mother, the inability to be truly present or vulnerable, really belonged more to her father.

Chapter 32

The thirty-second chapter is set in 1998 and discusses Robert Freedman's advances in his research on schizophrenia.

Robert Freedman had been meeting the Galvin boys throughout the 1990s as part of his research on sensory gating and vulnerability, his findings on schizophrenia brains having difficulty pruning information.

Eventually, Freedman discovered that schizophrenia patients had an issue with their $\alpha7$, or alpha-7, nicotinic receptor, and he tracked down the precise location where the problem took place: a chromosome that was home to a gene called CHRNA7, which the body uses to make the $\alpha7$ receptor. He was able to develop a drug that relieved patients from their delusions for days, but unfortunately, no company wanted to buy his patent as it was just a few years away from expiring. The drug also had to be taken several times a day, and therefore pharmaceutical companies saw no financial incentive in developing the drug as this made it unmarketable.

For Freedman, this was an object lesson in how pharmaceutical companies worked. He was back where he started and would have to find another way to jump-start the α7 receptor and strengthen the brain's ability to process information.

Chapter 33

The thirty-third chapter is set in 2000 and focuses on Lynn DeLisi and how she, like Robert Freedman, learned the hard way about the vagaries of the marketplace in pharma.

In 1995, after a decade of research on schizophrenia, DeLisi attracted the attention of a well-funded investor: Sequana Therapeutics, a privately held pharmaceutical company that would eventually partner with Parke-Davis to develop schizophrenia drugs.

DeLisi seemed poised for a breakthrough until Parke-Davis was bought by Pfizer, and her project was canceled.

There were many reasons for this, but the main reason was that Pfizer found it hard to financially justify spending money to develop something new when Thorazine and its offshoots were effective, stable, and had been around for so long that almost every company had its own version. Or, in other words: there was, again, not enough financial incentive.

Chapter 34

The thirty-fourth chapter revolves around Peter and his electroconvulsive therapy (ECT).

Peter's current diagnosis was bipolar disorder, and Lindsay had given up her legal guardianship so that he would be treated as a ward of the state, allowing him to stay for long periods at state hospitals if needed.

As a ward of the state, his doctors could petition the court on his behalf, and they decided to make use of ECT on a long-term basis, despite the potential risks involved.

Chapter 35

The thirty-fifth chapter discusses the deaths of Don, Jim, and Joe.

Jim died in 2001 due to a heart failure which was related to his use of neuroleptic drugs. His family took this to mean that he died of a condition called neuroleptic malignant syndrome—a rare, life-threatening disorder most often caused by the drugs meant to help. Margaret and Lindsay saw this as the cure being as bad as the disease, and they wondered if Donald, Joe, Matt, and Peter would be next.

Two years later, Don died of cancer. And in 2009, Joe died due to heart failure caused by clozapine intoxication. The powerful atypical neuroleptic had proven helpful to Joe in some ways, but the drug's physical side effects seemed to slowly wear his body down. The echoes of Jim's death were unmistakable.

Chapter 36

The thirty-sixth chapter is set in 2009. It discusses the advances in the research on schizophrenia.

After having been estranged from her research for nine years, Lynn DeLisi was contacted by Stefan McDonough, a neurobiologist who was working for Amgen, one of the world's largest biotechnology companies.

Together, they worked on a new schizophrenia study with her old samples, and thanks to the new and advanced technologies, they soon discovered that every Galvin brother from whom DeLisi had collected samples shared a mutation in a gene called SHANK2.

This showed that the same genetic determinants could lead to subtly different diseases, and discoveries like the

Galvin family's mutation could point the way toward a completely new conception of mental illness.

In 2010, the psychiatrist Thomas Insel, then director of NIMH, insisted on redefining schizophrenia as "a collection of neurodevelopmental disorders" instead of one single disease. The end of schizophrenia as a monolithic diagnosis could end the stigma surrounding the condition. What if schizophrenia was not a disease at all, but a symptom?

The second surprising revelation was about Mimi. For decades, Mimi had insisted that the family illness came from Don's side and she thought that his depression proved it. But while SHANK2 is not a sex-specific gene, this SHANK2 mutation came from the mother's side.

It could also be that Mimi's mutation was mingling with something on Don's side, which would mean that the genetic flaw that caused schizophrenia was caused by both of them together, a truly original mix, powerful enough to change all of their lives.

Chapter 37

The thirty-seventh chapter revolves around Robert Freedman's advances in his research on schizophrenia.

While Lynn DeLisi followed the trail of the SHANK2 gene, Robert Freedman continued his work with the CHRNA7 gene, and thanks in part to his work with the Galvins, Freedman had arrived at a game-changing strategy for the prevention of schizophrenia: choline, an essential nutrient that could help an at-risk child's brain to develop healthily, when it otherwise would not.

It had taken him thirty years, and only time could say for sure what difference choline could make, but the results were promising, and Freedman received the Lieber Prize for Outstanding Achievement in Schizophrenia Research.

Chapter 38

The thirty-eighth chapter is about Mimi, Margaret, and Lindsay and their current relationship.

None of the boys lived with Mimi anymore. Donald moved to assisted living three years earlier after Mimi suffered a stroke and was too frail to care for him by herself. This saddened Mimi, but she still saw all of the boys regularly.

Mimi opened up, but she remained aversive to self-reflection. Although Margaret felt sympathy for her mother, she also remained highly critical of her and how everything in her life was centered around Donald and the sick boys.

While Lindsay took it upon her to care for her brothers and mother, Margaret helped from a distance by sending gift cards and propping her sister up on the phone. In 2017, Mimi had another stroke and she had to stay at home under hospice care.

At first, both Margaret and Michael helped Lindsay to take care of their mother, but Margaret had a trip scheduled and left after some weeks. This is when the sick boys came back to visit; first Matt, then Peter, and finally Donald. In a flash, Lindsay was ten years old again and she felt abandoned and deserted, just as when she was left behind at home when Margaret went to live with Nancy Garcy.

Lindsay was furious with her sister as well as with any other family member who did not come to see Mimi, like Mark, Richard, and John.

Chapter 39

The thirty-ninth chapter revolves around Mimi's last weeks.

After having had a full-blown seizure, Lindsay, Jeff, and Michael took turns sleeping and sitting with Mimi. As they knew her end was nearing, Lindsay went to get Peter, Donald, and Matt to give them a chance to say goodbye.

Mark and Richard also came, and John was planning on coming a week later. Margaret, on the other hand, said that she had made her peace already and that she would not make the three-hour drive to see Mimi one more time.

Chapter 40

The fortieth chapter revolves around Lindsay and how she continued to take care of her sick brothers, as well as Mimi's funeral.

The night before Mimi's funeral, a dinner was held at Hidden Road Valley. Of the healthy siblings, only Richard and Margaret did not show up. Richard had fought over Mimi's will, and Margaret had told Lindsay that she did not want to spend the night at the house and that she only wanted to attend the funeral the next morning with Wylie and her two girls. Once again, Lindsay felt abandoned.

Part 3

Chapter 41

The forty-first chapter revolves around Lindsay and how she discovered more of her family's secrets.

Lindsay had left Hidden Valley Road when she was thirteen, determined never to come back. But now, with Mimi gone, she was back more often, checking in on Donald, Matt, and Peter, and prepping their parent's house for sale.

During one of her visits to Colorado Springs, Lindsay visited the state mental hospital in Pueblo where she discovered a few more family secrets while going through her brothers' old medical records, such as Donald's suicide attempt when he was twelve, as well as his attempt to kill himself and his wife with cyanide. An attempted murder-su-icide, like Brian had done three years later.

She could not help but wonder what might have changed if her parents had been more forthcoming about Donald. Could someone have prevented Brian from doing what he did?

Lindsay found paperwork on all of her brothers, as well as a file about her father who had apparently been having regular ECT sessions.

Although the secrecy made her sad, Lindsay hoped her family's story would at least make life better for others. With Robert Freedman's choline trials and Lynn DeLisi's SHANK2 revelations, at least there was a chance that her family's sac-rifice would help future generations.

Chapter 42

The forty-second chapter discusses Margaret's life, from her time at the Garys to her current life with Wylie, a man she considers her safe harbor.

Just like Mimi used to do, Margaret started painting more often. It became an emotional outpouring for her, and it helped her to deal with all of her traumas and emotions.

Both Brian's death and the sexual abuse were severely traumatic events, but the trauma Margaret dwelled on most often was abandonment—not just having been sent away to the Garys, but also constantly having been neglected in favor of her other siblings.

Chapter 43

The forty-third chapter discusses how schizophrenia is viewed and handled in this day and age.

Kolker wonders if the Galvin boys would have had a very different life if they had been born half a century later, and he notes that in some respects, little has changed. The market for new schizophrenia medicine remains sluggish, and the same nature-nurture squabbles have continued. Where the conversation once was about Freud, now it is about epigenetics—latent genes activated by environmental triggers. Researchers have come up with a variety of suspects, all of which have their adherents and detractors.

The grave dilemma of neuroleptic drugs also remains the same: medication, taken regularly, can stave off further breakdowns (while risking long-term side effects), but there is also ample evidence that patients who remain on drug regimens relapse as often as those who do not. While the surviving Galvin brothers are entirely dependent on neuroleptics by now, hopefully, medication and therapy will not be an either/or choice for future generations.

In fact, a relatively new wave of research supports the effectiveness of so-called "soft interventions", a more holistic approach that consists of talk therapy and family support, designed to keep the amount of medication to a minimum.

Another significant change is that more people are acknowledging the elusive quality of schizophrenia diagnoses. People are aware that there is no one-size-fits-all definition, and more and more evidence show that psychosis exists on a spectrum, with new genetic studies showing an overlap between different mental illnesses and disorders.

There are also some subtle changes. For example, the anti-psychiatry movement has become more concerned with legitimizing and normalizing the concept of hallucinations, and there is now a robust anti-medication movement that has gathered proof that shows that many schizophrenia patients experience favorable long-term outcomes without prescription drugs. This movement has support from many therapists who are unhappy with the notion of psychiatry as a pill mill.

Chapter 44

The forty-fourth chapter revolves around Margaret and Lindsay's squabble.

The sisters barely talked after Mimi's memorial, and it took them six months to try bridging the gap.

During this time, Lindsay came to some insights about what it is to be human. She used to talk about nature and nurture with her mother. Mimi, who was still wary of being judged, always insisted, defensively, that the illness was genetic, whereas Lindsay was not so sure of that.

Now Lindsay was finally getting closer to seeing how nature and nurture work together. She realized her mother was partially right. Biology is destiny, to a point, that cannot be denied; but what Lindsay also understood now, is that we humans are more than just our genes. To Lindsay, we are all, in some way, a product of the people who surround us. And while relationships can destroy us, they also have the power to change us and restore us. Without us ever seeing it happen, they end up defining us. We are human because the people around us make us human.

Chapter 45

The forty-fifth chapter introduces us to Kate and Jack, Lindsay's children.

Both Kate and Jack showed some signs of potential schizophrenia as children, but through early interventions and thanks to the help of the Garys, both children ended up thriving.

It made Lindsay wonder what would have happened to her sick brothers if there would have been something similar available at the time.

Kolker ends the book with Kate's visit to Robert Freedman's laboratory in 2017. Kate wanted to be a researcher and focus on schizophrenia, her family illness. At just eighteen, she was allowed to work as an intern at his lab, a highly sought-after position.

About *Hidden Valley Road: Inside the Mind of an American Family*

Hidden Valley Road is a testament to the entire Galvin family's generosity, candor, and faith that their story can be a help to others.

Robert Kolker was first introduced to Margaret and Lindsay in 2016. The two sisters were glad to finally have found a way to let the world know about their family. However, some requirements had to be met to do their story justice: every living Galvin family member would have to participate, and Kolker would need the independence to follow the story in any direction.

To be able to write *Hidden Valley Road*, Kolker spent hundreds of hours interviewing every living member of the

Galvin family (including Mimi Galvin, before her death in 2017), as well as dozens of friends, neighbors, researchers, teachers, therapists, colleagues, caregivers, and relatives. Not a single scene in the book was fabricated or invented, and all dialogue was either witnessed and recorded by Kolker or based on published accounts or the recollections of sources who were present at the time.

Additional resources were used to put together the family narrative, including, most notably, extensive interviews with researchers Lynn DeLisi, Robert Freedman, and Stefan McDonough; all available medical records for Don Galvin and his sons; Don's military service records; personal correspondence written by Mimi and Don; a series of recorded interviews with Mimi, conducted by Margaret in 2003 and 2008; and multiple entries from Margaret's diaries and autobiographical essays.

Margaret offered up decades of personal journals and diaries and biographical essays, sharing priceless details about life on Hidden Valley Road. Lindsay, in turn, worked tirelessly to locate medical records that no one knew still existed, filing paperwork, and connecting with numerous mental-health professionals and hospital administrators.

About the Book Cover

The cover of the book is a picture of the Galvin family at the U.S. Air Force Academy. It is one of the few group pictures that the family has and was taken in 1961. At the time, Peter was still a baby and Margaret and Lindsay were not born yet. The people that are seen in the picture are thus Mimi, Don, and their ten boys.

About Robert Kolker

Robert Kolker is a New York Times best-selling author and journalist.

His work has appeared in numerous magazines (such as The New York Times Magazine, New York Magazine, Wired, GQ, O, Bloomberg Businessweek, The Oprah Magazine, and Men's Journal), and he has received several awards.

His writing style is unadorned yet descriptive, and his work often takes the form of gripping, humane narratives.

Lost Girls, his famous crime book, was named one of the New York Times' 100 Notable Books. It recounts the lives of five sex workers who were murdered by the as-yet-unidentified Long Island serial killer. The book received wide critical acclaim and has been adapted for the 2020 feature film *Lost Girls*.

In 2004, Kolker published a story in New York Magazine about a public-school embezzlement scandal. This story was later adapted for the feature film *Bad Education*, starring Hugh Jackman. Two years later, he launched an investigation into sexual abuse in the ultra-Orthodox Jewish community. This investigation brought an abuser to justice and was nominated for a National Magazine Award. Through his exploration of an old murder exoneration case, Kolker was able to bring to light the police tactics that can lead to false confessions. For this, he received the Harry Frank Guggenheim 2011 Excellence in Criminal Justice Reporting Award from the John Jay College of Criminal Justice.

Trivia Questions

1. Who introduced Mimi and Don to falconry?

2. What was schizophrenia originally called?

3. What was Don's job after leaving the Navy?

4. What was Frieda Fromm-Reichmann's view on schizo-phrenia?

5. What were the names of Jim's wife and son?

6. Why were the Genian quadruplets not a great sample for the research on schizophrenia?

7. Where was the state mental hospital located where most of the boys were hospitalized?

8. What was the name of Brian's band?

9. What were "delusions" according to Jean-Paul Sartre?

10. Who were the four so-called hockey brothers?

11. Who witnessed Don having a stroke?

12. Why did Lynn DeLisi become so interested in researching schizophrenia?

13. What was the name of the housekeeper who worked for the Garys?

14. How did Lindsay, otherwise known as Mary, end up with her therapist, Louise Silvern?

15. What did John do for a living?

16. Which book about schizophrenia did Mimi start citing, and why?

17. Which family members received electroconvulsive therapy, or ECT?

18. What did Robert Freedman discover about the CHRNA7 gene?

19. What is neuroleptic malignant syndrome, and what causes it?

20. What is "psychosis" according to the epidemiologist John McGrath?

21. What are the names of Margaret's children?

22. Why did Richard have such a romanticized view of his father?

23. Why did Lindsay want to expose her children to her mentally ill brothers?

Congratulations

on finishing this book!

We hope that you have found this summary **valuable** and had an **enjoyable reading experience**.

We always **strive to improve** ourselves to **deliver the highest quality of work** to you.

But **we cannot improve without you**. If you like our efforts, **please support us** by giving us a quick review of the summary in our Amazon page by visiting the link or by scanning the QR code below. Your support will allow us to produce products of even **better quality** in the future.

https://link.intensivelife.com/HVRSummary

Thank you!

The Intensive Life Publishing Team

About Intensive Life Publishing

We live in a fast-paced world; everyone is always doing something. We started *Intensive Life Publishing* so that we can help people **get key ideas fast**. Our mission is to provide you with **accurate, well-written summaries** of some of the world's best-selling books so that you, as our reader, can **get the valuable information that you need**. This also, in turn, promotes those fantastic, best-selling books and their respective authors.

To know more about Intensive Life Publishing, you can visit **intensivelife.com** and **follow us** on social media:

 @intensivelifepublishing

@intensive_life

Made in the USA
Coppell, TX
25 April 2026

76584505R00066